UNVEILING THE ANOINTING

A Journey into Divine Empowerment

Benjamin Wordson

TABLE OF CONTENT

Chapter 1: Introduction

In the biblical context, the concept of the Anointing has deep roots that stretch across the Old and New Testaments. This chapter provides an overview of the Anointing, its historical and cultural significance, and its relevance in the biblical narrative.

Understanding the Anointing: Defining the Concept

The term "Anointing" originates from the Hebrew word "mashach" and the Greek word "chrio," both of which mean "to smear" or "to rub with oil." In the Bible, the Anointing is the act of consecrating or setting apart a person, object, or place for a sacred or holy purpose. It involves the application of oil, often infused with fragrant spices, as a symbolic act of endowing divine favor, power, or blessing.

The Anointing serves as a symbol of divine election, empowerment, and consecration. It signifies God's choice and approval of an individual for a specific role or purpose. Throughout the biblical narrative, the Anointing is closely associated with kings, priests, prophets, and even objects like the Tabernacle and the Ark of the Covenant.

Historical Perspectives on the Anointing in Various Religions

The Anointing is not unique to the Judeo-Christian tradition. Many ancient cultures and religions practiced anointing rituals. In the Bible, we can see examples of this in neighboring cultures, such as the anointing of kings in Mesopotamia.

One of the most famous biblical stories involving anointing is the anointing of David by the prophet Samuel. This event signifies a transition of power and God's divine choice of David as the future king of Israel, replacing Saul. It demonstrates how the Anointing was used to designate leadership and convey God's divine favor.

The Anointing's Role in Spiritual and Personal Development

Beyond its ceremonial aspects, the Anointing is also a spiritual concept that symbolizes the empowering presence of God's Spirit in the life of an individual. In the New Testament, particularly in the writings of the Apostle Paul, we find references to the Anointing of the Holy Spirit. This spiritual Anointing is seen as equipping believers with gifts and empowerment for their roles within the Christian community and the world.

The Anointing is not limited to leaders or special individuals; it is available to all believers who seek a deeper relationship with God. It plays a vital role in personal development, helping individuals fulfill their God-given potential and calling.

In this introductory chapter, we set the stage for a comprehensive exploration of the Anointing in the Bible, from its origins and historical context to its spiritual significance. As we journey through the subsequent chapters, we will delve deeper into the stories, rituals, and teachings that illuminate the concept of the Anointing in the biblical narrative.

Chapter 2: The Origins of the Anointing

Biblical Roots of the Anointing: An Exploration of Anointed Figures

The origins of the Anointing in the Bible can be traced back to the early narratives of the Old Testament. Anointing was a ritualistic practice that held significant spiritual and symbolic meaning. This chapter explores key figures in the Bible who were anointed and the profound implications of their anointing.

Anointing of Prophets: In the Old Testament, prophets were often anointed for their divine calling. One notable example is the prophet Elisha, who was anointed by the prophet Elijah as his successor (1 Kings 19:16). This transfer of the Anointing symbolized the continuation of God's prophetic work through a chosen vessel.

Anointing of Priests: Priests in ancient Israel were anointed to consecrate them for their sacred duties. Aaron, the brother of Moses, was anointed as the first high priest (Exodus 29:7). This act of anointing signified his role as an intermediary between the people and God, emphasizing the importance of purity and sanctification in priestly service.

Anointing of Kings: The anointing of kings was a pivotal event in Israel's history. Saul, the first king of Israel, was anointed by the prophet Samuel (1 Samuel 10:1). Later, David, a shepherd boy, was anointed by Samuel to be the future king (1 Samuel 16:13). This marked a divine choice and a transfer of authority, illustrating God's sovereignty over the nation and its leaders.

Anointing of Objects: The Anointing was not limited to individuals; it extended to sacred objects. The Tabernacle, its furnishings, and the Ark of the Covenant were anointed to consecrate them for divine service (Exodus 30:26-29). This practice highlighted the holiness of these items and their significance in worship.

Anointing in Other Sacred Texts and Traditions

While the concept of anointing is prominent in the Hebrew Bible, it is not unique to Judaism. Many ancient cultures and religions practiced anointing as a means of consecration, purification, and empowerment.

In ancient Egypt, for instance, anointing was used in mummification and in the coronation of pharaohs. Similarly, in Mesopotamia, anointing rituals were performed in various religious ceremonies and for healing purposes.

The presence of anointing practices in other cultures demonstrates the universal recognition of the symbolic power of oil and the significance of consecration.

Unraveling the Symbolism and Significance of Anointing Oil

Anointing oil, a central element in anointing ceremonies, holds deep symbolic significance. In the Bible, it represents the Holy Spirit and God's favor. The use of fragrant spices in the oil symbolizes the sweetness of God's presence.

In the New Testament, the concept of anointing with oil is extended to the anointing of believers with the Holy Spirit. This spiritual anointing empowers individuals for various ministries and service within the Christian community.

As we delve into the origins of the Anointing in this chapter, we gain a deeper appreciation for its rich history and significance in biblical narratives. It lays the foundation for our understanding of how anointing evolved and how it continues to be a potent symbol of divine calling and empowerment in both ancient and contemporary contexts.

Chapter 3: The Anointed and the Anointer

Recognizing the Anointer: Divine Sources of the Anointing

In the biblical context, the Anointer is most often understood to be God Himself. Anointing is a divine act, signifying God's choice, approval, and empowerment of an individual for a specific purpose. This chapter explores the biblical understanding of the Anointer and the divine sources of the Anointing.

God as the Ultimate Anointer: Throughout the Bible, God is portrayed as the ultimate source of the Anointing. When Samuel anointed Saul as king (1 Samuel 10:1) or David as king (1 Samuel 16:13), it was a manifestation of God's will. The prophet Nathan, under divine guidance, anointed Solomon as king (1 Kings 1:39). In these instances, the Anointing was a clear demonstration of God's choice and appointment.

The Holy Spirit as the Anointer: In the New Testament, the Anointer is often identified as the Holy Spirit. Jesus, before His earthly ministry, was anointed with the Holy Spirit at His baptism (Matthew 3:16). This Anointing empowered Him for His mission. In the early Christian community, believers received the Anointing of the Holy Spirit, equipping them for service and empowering them with spiritual gifts (Acts 2:1-4).

The Chosen Vessel: Characteristics of Anointed Individuals

Anointed individuals in the Bible exhibit specific characteristics and qualities that set them apart for their roles. This section explores some common traits of those anointed by God.

Faith and Obedience: Anointed figures often display deep faith and obedience to God's commands. Abraham, for example, was considered anointed in the sense that he was chosen by God for a special covenant (Genesis 12:1-3) due to his unwavering faith.

Humility and Dependence on God: Many anointed individuals demonstrate humility and a strong dependence on God. Moses, despite his reservations, accepted his anointed role as the leader of the Israelites (Exodus 4:10-12). He relied on God's guidance and power throughout his journey.

Courage and Resilience: Anointed individuals frequently face significant challenges and adversity. David, anointed as a young shepherd, displayed courage in defeating Goliath and resilience during his years of being pursued by King Saul.

The Process of Anointing:

Anointing ceremonies in the Bible follow a distinct process involving the use of anointing oil and the laying on of hands. This section provides insight into the observance aspects of anointing.

Anointing with Oil: The act of anointing typically involves the application of special oil, often infused with fragrant spices, onto the individual's head. This symbolizes the outpouring of God's Spirit upon the person.

Laying on of Hands: In some cases, anointing is accompanied by the laying on of hands. This physical touch represents the transference of authority, blessings, or empowerment. It's a gesture that signifies God's presence and favor.

Prophetic Declarations: Anointing ceremonies are often accompanied by prophetic declarations or words of blessing. These words serve to confirm the individual's calling and purpose in the eyes of God and the community.

In this chapter, we explore the roles of the Anointed and the Anointer in the biblical narrative. The Anointing is a divine act that signifies God's choice, empowerment, and approval of individuals for specific roles or purposes. Understanding the characteristics of anointed individuals and the process surrounding the Anointing provides valuable insights into the spiritual significance of this practice in the Bible.

Chapter 4: Empowering the Spirit

The Anointing and Spiritual Empowerment
The Anointing, as depicted in the Bible, plays a pivotal role in spiritual empowerment. It symbolizes the outpouring of God's Spirit upon an individual, equipping them for a specific purpose or ministry. This chapter explores the concept of the Anointing as a source of spiritual empowerment.

Divine Connection and Communion through Anointing: Anointing is often associated with a deep and intimate connection between the individual and God. It signifies a spiritual awakening or consecration, where the recipient becomes more attuned to God's presence and guidance. This connection is exemplified in the anointing of priests, who were required to maintain a high level of spiritual purity and communion with God.

Channeling the Anointing's Power for Positive Transformation: The Anointing is not merely a symbolic act; it carries a tangible empowerment. In the New Testament, Jesus was anointed with the Holy Spirit (Acts 10:38), which empowered Him for His earthly ministry. This Anointing enabled Him to perform miracles, heal the sick, and teach with authority. Similarly, believers in the early Christian community were anointed with the Holy Spirit, receiving spiritual gifts to edify the church and spread the Gospel (1 Corinthians 12:4-11).

Divine Gifts and Empowerment through the Anointing

The Anointing bestows divine gifts and abilities upon individuals, empowering them to fulfill their calling. These gifts may include wisdom, knowledge, discernment, prophecy, healing, and more. This section explores how the Anointing empowers individuals for service.

Prophetic Empowerment: Prophets in the Bible were often anointed to receive and deliver God's messages. The Anointing endowed them with the ability to perceive spiritual truths and foresee future events. For example, the prophet Isaiah received a profound vision of God's glory after being cleansed and anointed with a coal from the heavenly altar (Isaiah 6:1-8).

Healing and Miraculous Empowerment: The Anointing also played a role in healing and performing miracles. In the Old Testament, prophets like Elisha were anointed to heal the sick and perform supernatural acts. In the New Testament, the disciples, after receiving the Anointing of the Holy Spirit, healed the sick and performed miraculous deeds in the name of Jesus (Acts 3:1-10, Acts 5:12-16).

Empowerment for Leadership: Kings anointed by God were equipped with the wisdom and courage to lead their people effectively. Solomon, after his anointing as king, famously received wisdom from God, enabling him to make wise and just decisions (1 Kings 3:5-14).

The Anointing as a Transformative Experience

Anointing in the Bible is often accompanied by a transformative experience. The Anointing has the power to change an individual's perspective, character, and destiny. It is a divine catalyst for personal growth and spiritual development.

Transformation of Character: David, after being anointed by Samuel, was transformed from a humble shepherd into a valiant and wise king. His anointing marked the beginning of a journey of growth, challenges, and spiritual maturation.

Divine Guidance and Direction: The Anointing frequently leads individuals into their divine calling. Saul, after being anointed as king, received specific guidance and signs from God that directed him to his anointed destiny (1 Samuel 10:2-7).

In this chapter, we delve into the empowering nature of the Anointing as it relates to the human spirit. The Anointing represents a divine connection, equipping individuals with spiritual gifts and empowerment for service and personal transformation. It serves as a powerful force that enables individuals to fulfill their divine calling and make a positive impact on the world.

Chapter 5: Healing and Restoration

Anointing for Physical Healing: Traditions and Testimonies
The biblical narrative is replete with instances where the Anointing is associated with physical healing. This chapter explores the concept of anointing for physical healing, the traditions surrounding it, and the testimonies of miraculous recoveries.

Healing Oils and Balms: In the Bible, various oils and balms were used in healing rituals. The most famous is the story of the Good Samaritan who used oil and wine to care for the wounded traveler (Luke 10:34). Oil was seen as a soothing and medicinal substance. In the New Testament, the Apostle James encouraged the sick to call for the elders of the church, who would anoint them with oil and pray for their healing (James 5:14-15).

The Anointing Touch: In some instances, Jesus used touch as a means of healing. One remarkable account is the healing of the blind man, where Jesus mixed saliva with clay and anointed the man's eyes (John 9:1-7). This touch, infused with the Anointing, resulted in the man's miraculous sight restoration.

Testimonies of Healing: Throughout the Bible, there are numerous testimonies of individuals being healed through the Anointing. The stories of lepers being cleansed (2 Kings 5:1-14), the woman with the issue of blood (Mark 5:25-34), and the centurion's servant (Matthew 8:5-13) showcase the transformative power of the Anointing in physical healing.

Emotional and Psychological Restoration through the Anointing

The Anointing is not limited to physical healing; it also extends to emotional and psychological restoration. This section delves into instances where the Anointing was used to provide solace and healing for wounded hearts and minds.

David's Psalms of Healing: King David, himself an anointed figure, penned many psalms that reflect his deep emotional and spiritual struggles. These psalms, like Psalm 23, are often seen as expressions of his journey toward emotional and spiritual healing. They illustrate how the Anointing can provide comfort and restoration in times of distress.

The Anointing's Role in Forgiveness and Reconciliation: In the New Testament, a sinful woman anointed Jesus' feet with costly perfume and her tears (Luke 7:36-50). This act of devotion and repentance resulted in Jesus declaring her sins forgiven. It demonstrates the Anointing's role in facilitating forgiveness, reconciliation, and emotional healing.

Healing the World: Social and Environmental Impact of the Anointing

The Anointing is not limited to individual healing; it has the potential to bring healing and restoration to communities and even the environment.

Anointing for Social Justice: The Old Testament prophets, anointed to deliver God's messages, often spoke out against social injustices. They called for repentance, righteousness, and social reforms. Isaiah, for example, anointed to prophesy to the nations, often addressed issues of justice and the care of the marginalized (Isaiah 61:1-4).

Anointing for Environmental Stewardship: The Anointing also plays a role in advocating for the responsible stewardship of the Earth. The notion of anointing the land for fertility and abundance is found in the Bible (Deuteronomy 11:14). This reflects the belief that the Anointing can bring healing and restoration to the natural world.

In this chapter, we explore the multifaceted role of the Anointing in healing and restoration. Whether it's physical healing, emotional and psychological restoration, or addressing societal and environmental issues, the Anointing is portrayed as a potent force for positive transformation and renewal in the biblical narrative.

Chapter 6: Anointed Leadership

Anointed Leadership in Christian Organizations

In the biblical context, anointed leadership often holds a central place in christian organizations. This chapter explores how anointed leaders were chosen and their roles within these organizations.

Appointment of High Priests: In the Old Testament, the high priest was considered the highest religious authority among the Israelites. High priests, such as Aaron, were anointed to serve as intermediaries between the people and God. They played a crucial role in conducting sacrifices, rituals, and offering intercession for the nation.

Prophetic Leadership: Prophets in the Bible were anointed by God to deliver divine messages and guidance to the people. They served as spiritual leaders who often challenged the status quo and called for repentance and righteousness. Prophets like Samuel, Elijah, and Isaiah are prominent examples of anointed prophetic leadership.

Leadership in the Early Church: In the New Testament, anointed leadership continued in the early Christian church. Apostles and elders were appointed and anointed with the Holy Spirit to provide spiritual guidance, resolve disputes, and oversee the affairs of the growing Christian community (Acts 15:1-29).

Anointing and Political Leadership: Past and Present

In addition to religious leadership, anointed figures in the Bible often played significant roles in politics and governance. This section examines the intersection of anointing and political leadership.

Anointed Kings: The anointing of kings in the Old Testament was a profound political and religious event. It symbolized God's choice and endorsement of a leader to govern His people. Kings like David, Solomon, and Hezekiah were anointed to rule with wisdom, justice, and righteousness.

The Balance of Humility and Authority: Anointed leaders in the Bible were expected to balance humility with authority. King David, despite his anointing and authority, demonstrated humility by acknowledging his dependence on God and seeking His guidance (2 Samuel 7:18-29). This balance served as a model for anointed leadership.

Ethical Considerations and Accountability in Anointed Leadership

The Bible also addresses ethical considerations and the need for accountability in anointed leadership.

Leadership Accountability: Anointed leaders were held accountable to God and the people. When leaders strayed from their anointed path, they faced consequences. King Saul, for example, lost his anointing due to disobedience and pride (1 Samuel 15:10-11, 1 Samuel 16:14).

Shepherding God's Flock: Leaders were often described as shepherds of God's flock, tasked with caring for and protecting the people. The image of the shepherd emphasized the responsibility and care expected of anointed leaders (Psalm 23, Ezekiel 34:2-4).

Balancing Anointed Leadership with Servant Leadership

Anointed leadership in the Bible is closely associated with servant leadership. Leaders were anointed to serve God and His people, not to exercise power and authority for personal gain.

Jesus as the Ultimate Anointed Leader: Jesus is the ultimate example of anointed leadership. His ministry was characterized by humility, compassion, and service. He declared, "For even the Son of Man came not to be served but to serve, and to give his life as a ransom for many" (Mark 10:45).

Chapter 7: Anointing in Contemporary Society.

The Anointing in Modern Times: How it Persists

The concept of the Anointing, rooted in biblical traditions, continues to persist in contemporary society, albeit in evolving forms. This chapter explores how the Anointing has adapted and remained relevant in the modern world.

Anointing in Religious Practice: Christian maintain the practice of anointing with oil as a means of consecration and blessing. In Christianity, the Anointing of the Sick is a sacramental practice where the ill are anointed with oil for healing and spiritual comfort. James 5:14-15

Spiritual Empowerment and Renewal: The Anointing remains a symbol of spiritual empowerment and renewal in contemporary religious circles. Believers often seek the Anointing as a means of deepening their spiritual connection with God and receiving divine guidance.

Anointing in Worship and Practice: In Christian worship services, anointing with oil is sometimes part of special practices, such as baptism and confirmation. It is a way of invoking the presence of the Holy Spirit and consecrating individuals for their roles within the faith community.

Skepticism and Misuse of the Anointing's Power

While the Anointing is a cherished, contemporary society also witnesses skepticism and misuse of its power.

Charlatanism and Exploitation: Some individuals and groups exploit the concept of the Anointing for personal gain. Charlatans may claim to have special anointing powers to heal or provide blessings in exchange for financial support. This exploitation has led to skepticism and cynicism regarding anointing practices.

Discernment and Accountability: In response to misuse, there is a growing emphasis on discernment and accountability within religious communities. Leaders and practitioners are encouraged to exercise caution and discernment when claiming to possess the Anointing. Accountability measures are implemented to ensure ethical conduct.

Ethical Considerations and Accountability in Anointing Practices

Contemporary society places a premium on ethical considerations and accountability in anointing practices.

Transparency and Accountability: Religious organizations and leaders are expected to be transparent about their anointing practices. This includes explaining the purpose and scriptural basis for anointing ceremonies and being accountable for the use of funds and resources in connection with anointing services.

Balancing Faith with Prudence: Contemporary believers are encouraged to maintain a balance between their faith in the Anointing and prudence. This involves discerning genuine anointing practices from deceptive ones and seeking ethical, reputable leaders for spiritual guidance.

Anointing as a Personal Journey: Steps to Receiving and Growing in It

In contemporary society, many individuals embark on a personal journey of seeking the Anointing for their spiritual growth and empowerment.

Seeking a Deeper Spiritual Connection: People often seek the Anointing as a means of forging a deeper spiritual connection with the Holy Spirit. This may involve prayer and fasting, meditation, and participation in anointing services within their faith community.

Cultivating the Fruits of the Spirit: Growing in the Anointing is not merely about receiving power but also cultivating the fruits of the Spirit, such as love, joy, peace, patience, kindness, goodness, faithfulness, gentleness, and self-control (Galatians 5:22-23).

Service and Ministry: Those who receive the Anointing often feel called to serve and minister to others. This may involve community outreach, pastoral care, or participating in charitable activities.

In this chapter, we examine the continued presence of the Anointing in contemporary society. While its forms and practices have evolved, the core principles of spiritual empowerment, ethical conduct, and a personal journey of faith remain at the heart of the Anointing's significance in the modern world.

Chapter 8: Mysteries of the Anointing

Unraveling the Unexplained: Miracles and Supernatural Phenomena

The Anointing in the Bible is often associated with miracles and supernatural phenomena that defy natural explanations. This chapter delves into the mysterious and awe-inspiring aspects of the Anointing.

Healing Miracles: Throughout the Bible, we encounter accounts of miraculous healings through the Anointing. The mere touch of an anointed hand or the application of anointing oil could bring about instant healing. These stories challenge our understanding of the natural world and point to the miraculous power of the Anointing.

Supernatural Provision: In the Old Testament, we find stories of supernatural provision linked to the Anointing. The widow's jar of oil and flour miraculously refilling (1 Kings 17:8-16) or the multiplication of oil in the Shunammite woman's house (2 Kings 4:1-7) are examples of how the Anointing defies the laws of scarcity and sustains those under its influence.

Protection from Harm: The Anointing is sometimes portrayed as providing protection from harm. The anointing of David as a young shepherd is followed by his fearless confrontation with a lion and a bear (1 Samuel 16:13, 1 Samuel 17:34-37). These episodes illustrate the supernatural courage and protection that accompanied the Anointing.

Divine Revelation and Prophecy through the Anointing

Another mysterious facet of the Anointing is its connection to divine revelation and prophecy. Anointed individuals often receive visions, dreams, and prophetic insights.

Prophetic Dreams: Joseph, son of Jacob, had prophetic dreams that foretold his rise to power and the future of his family (Genesis 37:5-10). These dreams were connected to his destiny as an anointed leader.

Visions of the Heavenly Realm: Prophets like Ezekiel and Daniel had visions of the heavenly realm and received messages from God that revealed future events (Ezekiel 1:1, Daniel 7:1). These visions were often accompanied by a profound sense of the Anointing's presence.

Prophetic Utterances: The Anointing often led to prophetic utterances. The prophet Balaam, though initially resistant, was compelled by the Anointing to speak words of blessing over Israel (Numbers 24:1-9).

Embracing the Unfathomable: The Limitlessness of the Anointing

The Anointing, as portrayed in the Bible, knows no bounds. It is limitless in its potential for transformation and impact.

Anointing Across Generations: The Anointing is not confined to a single generation. It can be passed down, as seen in the anointing of Elisha by Elijah (1 Kings 19:16). This passing of the Anointing highlights its enduring power.

Anointing in Diverse Contexts: The Anointing is not restricted to religious or spiritual contexts. It can manifest in various life situations, from leadership and healing to creative endeavors and problem-solving. Its versatility showcases its boundless nature.

Anointing for Global Change: The Anointing has the potential to bring about global transformation. In the Old Testament, the Anointing of Cyrus, a Persian king, was prophesied by Isaiah to bring about the liberation of the Jewish exiles (Isaiah 45:1-3). This illustrates how the Anointing can work through unexpected channels to bring about significant change.

In this chapter, we explore the mysteries of the Anointing that transcend our understanding of the natural world. The Anointing is associated with miracles, divine revelations, and prophecy, and its limitless nature suggests that it can bring about profound and far-reaching transformations in the lives of individuals and even on a global scale.

Chapter 9: Cultivating the Anointing Within

Developing Spiritual Sensitivity and Discernment

Cultivating the Anointing within oneself begins with developing spiritual sensitivity and discernment. This chapter explores the process of attuning oneself to the presence and leading of the Holy Spirit.

Spiritual Sensitivity: Cultivating the Anointing requires heightened spiritual sensitivity. This involves learning to listen to the still, small voice of the Holy Spirit, which often communicates through inner promptings, intuition, and a sense of peace or conviction.

Discernment: Discernment is the ability to distinguish between the promptings of the Holy Spirit and other influences. It involves testing the spirits to ensure that what one perceives aligns with biblical truth and the character of God.

Anointing as a Personal Journey: Steps to Receiving and Growing in It

Receiving and growing in the Anointing is a personal journey that involves several key steps.

Seeking God's Presence: Cultivating the Anointing begins with seeking God's presence through prayer, meditation, and worship. Spending time in His presence opens the heart to receive His Anointing.

Living a Surrendered Life: Surrender is a fundamental aspect of cultivating the Anointing. It involves yielding one's will to God and allowing Him to shape one's character and desires. Surrender is often marked by humility and a desire to serve.

Walking in Obedience: Obedience to God's commands is a crucial step in growing in the Anointing. Obedience demonstrates faithfulness and trust in God's guidance.

Developing Spiritual Disciplines: Engaging in spiritual disciplines such as studying Scripture, fasting, and practicing gratitude can help individuals draw closer to God and foster a deeper Anointing.

Overcoming Obstacles and Doubts on the Path of the Anointing

The journey of cultivating the Anointing is not without its challenges and doubts. This section explores common obstacles and strategies for overcoming them.

Overcoming Self-Doubt: Many individuals struggle with self-doubt and feelings of inadequacy. The Anointing does not depend on human worthiness but on God's grace. Believers must learn to trust in God's choice and plan for them.

Resisting the World's Distractions: The world is filled with distractions that can hinder the cultivation of the Anointing. Prioritizing spiritual pursuits over worldly distractions is essential.

Persevering in Faith: The journey of cultivating the Anointing often requires perseverance in the face of challenges and setbacks. Faith in God's promises and the power of the Anointing can help individuals overcome difficulties.

Cultivating a World Guided by Divine Empowerment

As individuals cultivate the Anointing within themselves, they become agents of transformation in the world.

Empowering Others: Those who have cultivated the Anointing are often called to empower and mentor others on their spiritual journey. This includes passing down the Anointing and sharing insights and experiences.

Impact on Society: The Anointing has the power to impact society positively. It can lead to acts of justice, compassion, and social transformation.

Creating a World Guided by Divine Empowerment: Ultimately, cultivating the Anointing within oneself contributes to the creation of a world guided by divine empowerment, where individuals are empowered to fulfill their God-given purposes and work for the betterment of humanity.

In this chapter, we explore the personal journey of cultivating the Anointing within oneself. It involves developing spiritual sensitivity, walking in obedience, overcoming obstacles, and ultimately becoming an agent of positive change in the world through the power of the Anointing.

Chapter 10: Anointing and Unity

The Anointing as a Unifying Force

The Anointing, as portrayed in the Bible, has the potential to serve as a unifying force within communities and societies. This chapter explores how the Anointing fosters unity among individuals, families, and communities.

Common Spiritual Experience: The Anointing often leads individuals to share a common spiritual experience. Believers who have received the Anointing of the Holy Spirit, for example, may describe a sense of unity and fellowship as they worship and serve together. This shared experience creates bonds that transcend differences and foster unity.

One Body, Many Parts: The New Testament likens the body of believers to a single body with many parts, each having a unique function (1 Corinthians 12:12-27). The Anointing is what empowers and unifies these diverse individuals for the common purpose of advancing God's kingdom.

Empowering Unity in Diversity: The Anointing has the power to bring unity in the midst of diversity. The early Christian community, composed of Jews and Gentiles with different backgrounds and cultures, experienced a unifying Anointing that transcended these differences (Ephesians 2:14-16).

Anointing Leaders for Unity and Service

Anointed leaders play a crucial role in fostering unity within their communities. This section explores how leaders anointed by God can serve as catalysts for unity.

Serving as Role Models: Anointed leaders are often seen as role models of unity and humility. They exemplify Christ-like qualities that inspire others to follow their lead in pursuing unity and harmony.

Building Bridges of Understanding: Anointed leaders are skilled in building bridges of understanding and reconciliation. They mediate conflicts and seek common ground among diverse individuals or groups.

Empowering Others for Service: Anointed leaders empower others within their community for service. They recognize and nurture the unique gifts and callings of individuals, which contributes to the overall unity and effectiveness of the community.

Anointing for Healing and Reconciliation

The Anointing is often associated with healing and reconciliation, both of which are essential components of unity.

Healing Wounds: The Anointing has the power to heal emotional and relational wounds. It can bring forgiveness, restoration, and healing to individuals and communities torn by conflict or division.

Reconciling Differences: Anointed individuals are often called to reconcile differences and promote unity. They may mediate disputes, facilitate dialogue, and encourage forgiveness.

Anointing and Global Unity

The Anointing is not limited to individual or community unity; it also has the potential to contribute to global unity.

Anointing for Global Change: Anointed leaders and individuals are often at the forefront of global initiatives for positive change. They work to address issues such as poverty, injustice, and environmental concerns, bringing diverse groups together for a common cause.

Uniting in Prayer and Purpose: Anointed individuals and communities often unite in prayer for global issues and challenges. This collective prayer and action can lead to transformative change on a global scale.

In this chapter, we explore how the Anointing serves as a unifying force within individuals, families, communities, and even on a global level. It empowers leaders to foster unity, heal wounds, and reconcile differences, ultimately contributing to a world marked by harmony, compassion, and collaboration.

Chapter 11: Leaving a Lasting Legacy

The Significance of Legacy in Biblical Context

Legacy, as understood in the Bible, holds great significance. It is the idea that one's actions, choices, and impact continue to influence and shape the world even after their time on Earth has ended. This chapter explores the biblical concept of legacy and how the Anointing plays a crucial role in leaving a lasting legacy.

Generational Blessings and Curses: The Bible often portrays the idea that the actions of one generation can have far-reaching consequences for their descendants. The Anointing, when used to fulfill God's purposes, can result in generational blessings, while disobedience can lead to generational curses (Exodus 20:5-6).

The Anointed David's Legacy: King David, anointed by God, left a lasting legacy. His legacy included the establishment of Jerusalem as the capital of Israel, the design of the temple, and the compilation of the Book of Psalms. David's lineage also led to the birth of Jesus Christ, the ultimate legacy of salvation for humanity.

The Anointing and Kingdom Building

The Anointing often involves a divine commission to build God's kingdom on Earth. This section explores how the Anointing is linked to the construction of a lasting kingdom.

Kingdom-Building Anointing: Kings and leaders in the Bible were anointed with a kingdom-building Anointing. They were entrusted with the responsibility of leading their people in God's ways and establishing just and righteous rule (2 Samuel 7:12-16).

Kingdom Impact: The Anointing empowers individuals to make a significant impact on the world. Prophets, like Isaiah and Jeremiah, were anointed to deliver messages that would shape the future of nations. Their words continue to influence generations.

Passing Down the Anointing

One aspect of leaving a lasting legacy is the passing down of the Anointing to the next generation. This involves mentoring and equipping successors to carry on the work of the Anointing.

Elisha and Elijah: The relationship between Elisha and Elijah serves as a powerful example of the passing down of the Anointing. Elijah anointed Elisha as his successor, and Elisha received a double portion of Elijah's Anointing (2 Kings 2:9-15).

Mentoring and Discipleship: Passing down the Anointing often involves mentoring and discipleship. Anointed leaders invest in the spiritual development and training of those who will carry on the work.

Anointed Legacy in the New Testament

The New Testament continues the theme of leaving an anointed legacy. This section explores how the Anointing in the New Testament is connected to the establishment and growth of the early Christian church.

Anointing of the Holy Spirit: In the New Testament, believers were anointed with the Holy Spirit, equipping them for ministry and service (Acts 2:1-4). This Anointing empowered them to spread the Gospel and build the early Christian church.

Paul's Ministry and Legacy: The Apostle Paul, anointed for his mission to the Gentiles, left a lasting legacy through his writings and the establishment of numerous churches. His epistles continue to guide and instruct believers in the faith.

Leaving a Christ-Centered Legacy

Ultimately, the most enduring legacy is one centered on Christ. The Anointing empowers individuals to proclaim the Gospel and lead others to a saving knowledge of Jesus Christ.

Pointing to Christ: The Anointing empowers believers to point others to Jesus Christ, who is the ultimate legacy of salvation and eternal life (John 3:16).

Perpetuating the Faith: Leaving a lasting legacy involves passing down the faith to future generations. Timothy, mentored by the Apostle Paul, is an example of the transmission of the Anointing and the faith to the next generation (2 Timothy 1:6).

In this chapter, we explore the concept of leaving a lasting legacy in the biblical context, emphasizing how the Anointing plays a pivotal role in building God's kingdom, mentoring successors, and perpetuating the faith for generations to come. A legacy grounded in the Anointing can have a profound and enduring impact on the world.

Chapter 12: Embracing the Anointing's Call

The Divine Calling of the Anointing

The Anointing, as depicted in the Bible, is often associated with a divine calling. This chapter explores the concept of the Anointing's call and the profound responsibility that accompanies it.

Chosen for a Purpose: Those who receive the Anointing are chosen for a specific purpose. Whether it's to lead a nation, prophesy to the people, or serve in a priestly role, the Anointing signifies a divine calling to fulfill a particular mission.

Anointed for Service: The Anointing is not a passive gift; it comes with the call to serve. Anointed leaders and individuals are called to serve God and their fellow human beings. This service may involve teaching, healing, prophesying, or any number of ministries.

Embracing the Anointing's Call: Steps to Fulfilling the Mission

Embracing the Anointing's call requires a deliberate response and commitment. This section explores the steps one must take to fulfill the mission bestowed by the Anointing.

Recognition and Acceptance: The first step is recognizing and accepting the Anointing's call. This often involves a sense of divine conviction or a confirmation through spiritual leaders or mentors.

Surrender and Obedience: Embracing the Anointing's call necessitates surrendering one's will and desires to God's plan. Obedience to God's leading is crucial in fulfilling the mission.

Preparation and Equipping: Preparation is essential to fulfilling the Anointing's call. This may involve formal education, training, or spiritual development. It also includes seeking God's guidance and wisdom for the journey.

Accountability and Mentorship: Being accountable to spiritual mentors and leaders is essential in embracing the Anointing's call. Mentorship provides guidance, encouragement, and accountability in the pursuit of the mission.

Challenges and Opposition on the Path of the Anointing's Call

Embracing the Anointing's call is not without its challenges and opposition. This section explores common obstacles that individuals may encounter.

Resistance and Rejection: Anointed individuals often face resistance and rejection, both from within their communities and from external forces. The prophet Jeremiah, for example, faced rejection and persecution as he delivered God's messages (Jeremiah 1:6-8).

Spiritual Warfare: The path of the Anointing's call often involves spiritual warfare. Believers may encounter spiritual opposition and challenges that require spiritual discernment and reliance on God's strength (Ephesians 6:12).

Testing and Refinement: Challenges and trials serve to refine those who embrace the Anointing's call. They test one's faith, character, and commitment to the mission.

Fulfilling the Anointing's Call for God's Glory

Ultimately, embracing the Anointing's call is a journey of faith and obedience that leads to the glorification of God.

Bringing Glory to God: Anointed individuals fulfill their missions to bring glory to God. Their actions, empowered by the Anointing, point to God's sovereignty, grace, and love.

Impact on Others: Embracing the Anointing's call often results in a positive impact on others. It can lead to the salvation of souls, the healing of the sick, the restoration of communities, and the transformation of lives.

In this chapter, we explore the profound calling of the Anointing and the steps one must take to embrace it. Embracing the Anointing's call is a journey marked by recognition, surrender, preparation, and accountability. It comes with challenges but ultimately leads to the fulfillment of a divine mission for God's glory and the betterment of humanity.

Conclusion: Embracing the Anointing's Divine Path

In this exploration of the Anointing, we have embarked on a journey through the pages of the Bible, uncovering the rich tapestry of its significance, mysteries, and transformative power. From the earliest accounts of anointing observance in the Old Testament to the outpouring of the Holy Spirit in the New Testament, the Anointing has been a central theme, woven into the fabric of divine encounters, spiritual empowerment, and the fulfillment of God's purposes.

We have seen how the Anointing serves as a divine mark of consecration, setting apart individuals for specific roles and missions. It is the sacred oil that empowers leaders, prophets, priests, and kings to carry out their God-ordained tasks with wisdom, authority, and spiritual insight.

The Anointing, as portrayed in the Bible, is not static but dynamic—a living force that transforms lives, heals the sick, restores the brokenhearted, and empowers believers for service. It is a wellspring of divine revelation, prophecies, and miracles that challenge the boundaries of the natural world, pointing to the infinite power and love of God the Creator.

We have also explored how the Anointing calls us to a personal journey of faith—a journey of spiritual sensitivity, discernment, and surrender. It beckons us to seek God's presence, live a surrendered life, and walk in obedience, trusting in His divine guidance. Along this path, we may encounter obstacles and opposition, but we are reminded that the Anointing equips us to overcome challenges and fulfill our divine callings.

The concept of legacy has also been a recurring theme, emphasizing that the Anointing's impact extends beyond our lifetime. Through the Anointing, we can leave a lasting legacy of faith, righteousness, and service that influences future generations, just as King David's legacy led to the birth of Jesus Christ, the ultimate legacy of salvation.

In concluding our exploration, we are reminded that the Anointing is not confined to the pages of ancient scripture but remains relevant in contemporary society. It continues to empower individuals and communities for service, healing, and transformation. Its role in fostering unity, reconciliation, and global change underscores its enduring significance.

As we embrace the Anointing's divine path, we are called to recognize its call, surrender to its leading, and persevere through challenges. We become agents of transformation in a world hungering for hope, healing, and restoration. Our lives become a testament to the boundless love and grace of our Creator, pointing others to the ultimate legacy— salvation through Jesus Christ.

May the Anointing guide your steps, empower your service, and inspire your faith as you continue your own journey, leaving a lasting legacy for God's glory and the betterment of humanity.

Note: The book, "Unveiling the Anointing: A Journey into Divine Empowerment," aims to explore the concept of the Anointing from various religious, spiritual, and historical perspectives. It delves into its origins, purpose, and power, as well as its relevance in contemporary society. The book encourages readers to discover and cultivate the Anointing within themselves and to use it for positive impact in the world. Through the pages of this book, readers will gain a deeper understanding of the Anointing's potential to inspire and empower humanity to embrace their higher calling and create a world guided by divine empowerment.

Note

Note

Note

Note

Books Of
Benjamin Wordson

Facebook:Benjamin Wordson
Instagram: Benjamin Wordson

www.benjaminwordson.org
Canada
2023

Made in the USA
Columbia, SC
13 September 2024

41407612R00033